Depósito Legal: MA. 764 - 1977   ISBN: 84-7224-062-2

THE CAVE OF NERJA

EDITED BY THE FOUNDATION OF THE CAVE OF NERJA

PABLO SOLO DE ZALDIVAR YEBENES

COLLABORATORS:

Anthropology:
RICARDO GARCES
MIGUEL FUESTE

Geology:
ANTONIO PEÑAS MALDONADO

Entomology:
ANTONIO COBOS

Photography:
ARCHIVES OF THE FOUNDATION

Drawings and plans:
HECTOR VELAZQUEZ

Special Collaboration:
MARIA VICTORIA RODRIGUEZ MARTIN

Direction

Ediciones albayzin

GRANADA

PROLOGUE TO THE FIRST EDITION

In the year 1959, in Nerja, the discovery took place of one of the archaeological beds that was to attract a great deal of attention for the impressive morphology it offered.

Although it was the stalactite and stalagmite formations which first attracted attention, it was from the scientific point of view that its interest augmented, for the bed has contributed a series of indexes and pointers which have allowed a very definite cultural sequence to be established.

The Provincial Delegation of Excavation of Málaga realised from the beginning the scientific importance that such a bed could have, and entrusted Doctor Pellicer, then Professor of the University of Granada, with the first organised work of archaeological investigation.

Encouraged by the results obtained, the Foundation of the Cave of Nerja decided to continue, and in view of the impossibility of Professor Pellicer assuming the direction, since he had other obligations, they entrusted the job to other experts from the National Service of Excavations for the General Management of the Arts.

Since the work carried out by Professor Pellicer and his collaborators, two more campaigns have been carried out up until now under the direction of Miss Ana María de la Quadra Salcedo, and her work has been crowned with great success, since it has permitted a considerable increase in our knowledge of the cultural heritage to be found in the cave. Remains of materials, work utensils and anthropological remains of singular importance have been brought to light in the new digs, and, whilst a study of other results is being prepared which gives still greater importance to the bed, it has been considered a good idea to make public the first results, obtained by Professor Pellicer, which demonstrate the great care which must be taken in dealing with this type of bed, so that nothing should be lost from the scientific point of view.

In this aspect the Cave of Nerja has been a lucky bed. From the very beginning, attention has been paid to it from the double angle of science and tourism, and the result of this double interest could not have been more satisfactory, as proved by the results already obtained and those still to come, because in view of what has already been achieved there are excellent motives for hoping for still more new and important discoveries in the core of this bed, whose fame has already crossed our frontiers.

The data accumulated during the first exploration in Nerja, although the results obtained were not exhaustive, as the work since carried out has proved, is of prime importance and cannot be detracted from in any way in view of its being carried out under truly heroic circumstances. For that reason it is only just that public recognition should be given to those who first called attention to the archaeological importance of this cave: Simeón Giménez Reyna, Juan Temboury, Pablo Sólo de Zaldívar, Eduardo Ortega, Ricardo Garcés, Sebastián Arrabal, Antonio Pezzi, Manuel Casamar, and Manuel Pellicer, as also to those others whose interest made it possible to turn the Cave of Nerja into a first class tourist centre, these last mentioned personified in the name of Antonio García y Rodríguez Acosta, Subsecretary of Tourism and Civil Governor of Málaga when the work was carried out, that made possible the easy access to the cave and its illumination; the Foundation which looks after the conservation and study of the bed was organised and the scientific lines to be followed laid down, these last being followed at the moment with the efficient help of Don Ramón Castilla Pérez, the present Civil Governor of the province of Málaga.

The work of exploration now being carried out, together with the work initially done, has made possible the scientific collection of important material which properly displayed in the interior of the cave itself allows the public to form some idea of the sequence of cultures that took place in this same cave, these running from paleolithic times up to modern history, showing that from very early on this Cave of Nerja has exercised a strong attraction for man, whatever the cultural ambiance in which he developed. This circumstance, together with the singular beauty offered by its morphology, makes the Cave of Nerja a scientific and tourist centre of special significance, since on many occasions in the future it will have to be used as the yardstick by which other beds are valued culturally speaking, and in trying to judge the tourist value of other places.

GRATINIANO NIETO GALLO
General Director of Fine Arts.

DECLARATION AS HISTORIC AND ARTISTIC MONUMENT

The "Official State Bulletin" number 142, of Thursday 15th of June 1961 by which the Cave of Nerja in Maro (Málaga) is declared an Historic and Artistic Monument:

"The Cave of Nerja in Maro (Málaga) recently discovered and to which such special attention has been paid by the Foundation which was originally organised for its care, is of singular natural beauty because of the stalactites and stalagmites which abound, but it also possesses a great historical interest because of the rupestrian paintings which exist therein and for the importance of the bed that exists in its subsoil.

"It is therefore necessary to give due importance to this bed and to endow it with all the most effective measures of protection of which the State disposes, in order to make known its significance, guarantee its conservation and undertake its scientific study.

"For the above reasons, after hearing the Royal Academy of Arts of San Fernando and the General Comissariat in the Service of the Defence of the National Artistic Patrimony and the due deliberation of the Council of Ministers, in their reunion of the twelfth day of May 1961.

I ORDER:

Article 1.   The Cave of Nerja in Maro (Málaga) is declared an Historic and Artistic Monument.

Article 2.   The care of this Monument, which remains under the protection of the State, will be undertaken by the Minister for National Education.

I order this through this present decree given out in Madrid on the twenty-fifth of May of nineteen hundred and sixty-one.

FRANCISCO FRANCO

The Minister of National Education,
Jesús Rubio García Mina

View of the gardens (Cantina)

PREFACE

By publishing this book on the Cave of Nerja, we are tying to offer the reader a brief panorama of its history. We want to make public some of the work of investigation carried out in it; to show, by means of graphic documentation, those corners which are unknown to the general public, and which, because of their situation, are impossible to see easily or comfortably. For example, there are the High Galleries with their halls and rupestrian paintings, that up until now we cannot foresse the moment of their incorporation as part of the visitable monument. Problems, due to the height which separates their rooms from the exterior or other viable points, make it impossible to carry out this project. These are the reasons which justify our dedicating as much space as is possible in a work of this type to this, without doubt, interesting theme.

The Cave of Nerja has two outstanding aspects in its favour which any study of the subject must emphasise: the monumental or tourist and the scientific or archaeological. The Foundation created a few days after its discovery has managed to combine both of these with good judgement, giving importance to both aspects to the point where the name of the Cave of Nerja has leapt our frontiers and become universally known.

We can neither forget nor fail to express our gratitude to the then Civil Governor of the province, His Excellency Don Antonio J. García Rodríguez-Acosta, founder and first president of the Foundation of the Cave of Nerja, and through him we wish to thank all those who have succeeded him in this post and have carried on the work that he began so well.

The two above mentioned themes, which will be referred to all through this work, can be resumed as follows: The Cave, situated in the extreme eastern corner of the province, where tourism had only arrived sporadically. constituted the "boom" of the first few years of the sixties, and made for the full incorporation of this zone in the tourist stream of the Costa del Sol, which before had been all but limited to Torremolinos and Marbella.

From the scientific point of view, it offers an archaeological bed that is completely intact, having been closed for 3.000 years, a fact, this, of great importance for the archaeology of Málaga, since, although there are other cave in the area, they have always been the object of pillage by fortune hunters, as is usual in such cases. The bed is protected by paving, which in the form of walks over the zone of interest, avoids the possibility of erosion exposing the pieces contained in the subsoil.

Monument to the Discovery of the Cave

View of Maro from the Cave

DISCOVERY

Near the old cemetery of Maro, there exists a shallow pond. This leads into a cavern from which at nightfall large flocks of bats fly. It is called the Mine.

One day, some boys from Maro and Nerja decided to hunt these animals, for which reason they were carrying the appropiate nets. They went into the cavern by way of the well and got ready for the hunt.

One of them became aware of a gentle warm draught, and they realised that it came from a narrow fissure of some sixty centimetres wide by one metre in height, but they could not get into it because two strong stalactites, like bars, blocked their entrance. They decided after several useless attempts to return the following day in the company of another friend from Maro, and, armed with a chisel and a hammer, so as to break them.

On the 12th of January 1959 they went back to the well, and, after some effort, managed to break the stalactites. There were then five boys in the expedition: José Luis Barbero de Miguel, Manuel and Miguel Muñoz Zorrilla, Francisco Navas Montesinos and José Torres Cárdenas. Navas Montesinos went headfirts through the hole and into the unknown.

Premios a los descubridores de la Cueva de Nerja

/ ver. en el Gobierno Civil, fueron distribuídas 400.000 pesetas en premios a los descubridores de la Cueva de Nerja. En la foto, el Gobernador civil, don Antonio García Rodríguez-Acosta, conversa con los jóvenes durante el simpático acto. (Véase información en página   .) (Foto Salas.)

Photograph published in the daily newspaper "Sur" of Málaga

He found the entrance to a very narrow chimney, the end of which he could see a little further on, and on arriving there he was lucky enough to find a projection from which he could jump to the floor; the others quickly followed him and a few metres further on they found that they could stand upright. A little later they came out, down an incline full of stones, into what is now known by the name of the Hall of the Cascade. They were in what is now the great cave (Hall IV) but the explorers saw very little, since their torches lost the force of their beam at very little distance, due to the great size of the cavern and the impenetrable darkness.

Work carried out to make the present entrance

By the 2nd of April 1960 it becomes possible for vehicles to reach the spot where the perforation, that today serves as the entrance to the Çave, had been carried out

Some skeletons lying in a corner with some bowls beside them frightened the boys and they left the Cave. On arriving back home, in great excitement, they told their teachers, Miss Mora Plaza and Mr. Carlos Saura, that they had found an enormous cave.

The subject of the cave appeared to have been forgotten about, in spite of the continual statements of its discoverers, until, on hearing the news, the Front for Youth of Nerja decided to undertake a new exploration. This expedition was joined by the doctor Sr. Garcés, and the photographer Sr. Padial, who thus also came to know the cave. Recognising its beauty, they decided to send the photographs they had taken to the daily newspaper "Sur" of Málaga, which, when it published them, in the number 7.373 of the 22nd of April 1959, with some preliminary information, attracted the attention of the Delegation for Archaeological Excavations of Málaga, which immediately became interested in this bed.

A few days later, this Delegation organised an excursion to Nerja and got into contact with the then Mayor, Sr. Millán, and Doctor Garcés, who showed them the entrance and the way through the cave.

It was found that the entrance, twisty and obviously dangerous because of its narrowness, did not permit the use of material appropiate to a thorough investigation, for which reason Mr. Solo de Zaldívar, a member of the Delegation, was given the difficult task of finding the original entrance, which must exist somewhere, or at least of making an artificial one which would allow easy access to the people and material necessary.

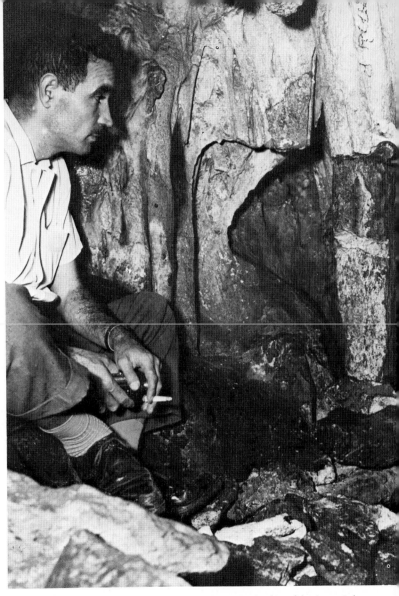

The hole made by the discoverers so as to be able to get in

It was necessary to climb a steep and slippery cascade of stalagmites more than 18 metres high and bury oneself in a series of smaller caves which inevitably ended in narrow passages with no way of exit to the outside. In one of such passages a large root was found and a plan was made from the entrance to this point, and later the exterior location of this same point. It was the root of a pine tree. Four metres underneath it was found what turned out to be the old entrance to the cave, which had been covered up by the effects of time.

The next day they started the vertical perforation at this spot. To open it was easy and it took only one blast of dynamite to move a large rock which completely blocked the entrance. Once free of this, for the first time in 3.000 years, daylight penetrated the hole to the great delight of all those present.

The Foundation of the Cave of Nerja agreed, soon after its creation in 1960, to give an important money prize to the discoverers and to pay for the studies they chose to undertake. The discoverers preferred to join the personnel working in the Cave, where some of them still continue to work.

Panorama of the urbanised zone and, in the background, the
town of Nerja

GEOGRAPHICAL SITUATION

The National road 340 Cádiz-Barcelona crosses the province of Málaga, and today constitutes the main artery of the famous Costa del Sol, at the extreme West of which lies Estepona, and at the East, Nerja. The capital city of Málaga is approximately in the middle, between these two points.

On leaving Málaga, going towards Almería, the road hugs the coast, sometimes along flat land and sometimes across higher points but always in view of the sea. It goes through country dedicated to orchards, sugar cane, vines, olives and in some places ones attention is attracted by huge expanses of nursery gardens of flowers and vegetables. In between these agricultural zones, residential areas have been created, always somewhere near one of the many villages that exist such as La Cala, Rincón de la Victoria, Benajarafe, Torre del Mar, Torrox and Nerja, just beyond which last, 4 kms. further on, just before coming to the little village of Maro, there is a road which leads to the entrance of the Cave, situated 300 metres above sea level and 700 from the littoral, embedded in the calcerous mesozoic rock which here runs parrallel to the coast.

Just near the entrance of the Cave of Nerja, are various buildings used for ticket offices, bar and restaurant facilities and shops.

That same date became an historic day for the Cave of Nerja when the then Civil Governor of the province, Don Antonio J. García Rodríguez Acosta, accompanied by other provincial and local authorities, visits the Cave for the first time and decided its future

The zone nearest the entrance has been perfectly urbanised and has large gardens, a children's playground, a bar, an open air dining room, parking for buses and cars, a shop which sells souvenirs as well as a restaurant, bar-cafeteria and a meteorological station.

In the gardens and next to the entrance pavilion of the Cave stands a monument dedicated to its discovery, the work of the sculptor Carlos Monteverde.

From the terraces of the bar and restaurant you have a marvellous view over Maro and Nerja, surrounded by fields of sugar cane and with the blue of the sea as a background.

To the North are the hills of Lucero 1.450 metres high, under which one day the Cave of Nerja started to form.

Situation Plan

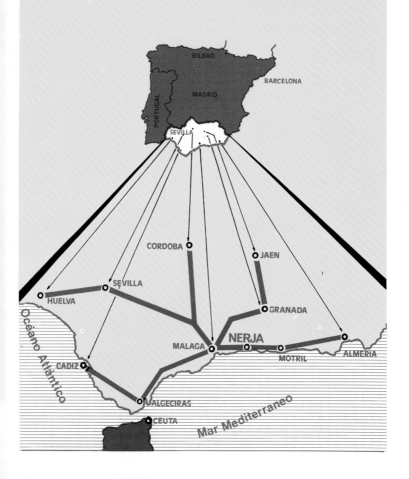

Nerja beach

DESCRIPTION

Access to the Cave is made by means of a staircase down to a hall fourteen metres long and three
high, whose floor is one enormous archaeological
bed. Here various archaeological explorations have
been carried out with one very important result which
we will mention later.

This first hall and the following one are joined by
a narrow corridor partly hewn out of the rock, as,
originally, it had to be passed on hands and knees;
this leads to the second fairly large hall, which is
twenty metres long, ten metres wide and five high.
This is called the Hall of the Nativity, because one
corner of it resembles very much the Stable at Beth-
lehem of our traditional Christmas. Beautifully lit pic-
turesque cavities surprise the visitor.

The Hall of the Nativity or Hall II communicates,
on its left, with another hall — Hall III called the
Hall of the Elephant's Tusk. In earlier publications
about the Cave of Nerja it said: "It got its name from
the tusk of an elephant found there in fossilised form;
this refers to a formation protected by glass. This
can be seen on the left hand side as you come into
the hall, at floor level."

It would as well to clarify that this formation never contained a tusk. As can be seen, it is completely hollow, and made of a layer of stalagmite that must have covered the object that gave it its shape. For this reason, we can be sure that that object was neither a tusk nor a bone, since the organic nature of these would not permit their decomposition in an atmosphere rich in calcerous concretions: it is suspected that it was probably a leaf with an arched shape, which, arriving in the cave already very dry, could have produced this formation. In spite of this, the name has remained more in its analogous sense than in its technical one.

This hall has a rich archaeological bed, partly explored on opening the new communication with the exterior, by making use of a natural chimney. This exit has been made in order to make the monument easier to visit.

From the Hall of the Elephant's Tusk one goes down — a staircase built on hard rock — until one comes out onto a sort of balcony which dominates, on the right, the Hall of the Cascade. From the balcony, halfway down this staircase, one gets the most marvellous view of the Cave. From here one can see as the entrance to the Hall of the Cataclysm, a view of two hundred metres.

At the end of this staircase, on the left, there is a diversion down which came the discoverers of the Cave.

We find ourselves now in Hall IV or the Hall of the Cascade, thus called because of the stalagmite pillars or "gours", a formation of great beauty. The

Hall of the Nativity

Hall of the Ghosts

height of the ceilings is of some twenty-five metres by thirty metres wide, some idea of its size can be got from the fact that the ballet festivals are held here with some six hundred spectators. In the floor of this Hall were found various jars and neolithic implements together with interesting anthropological remains.

By means of a wide passageway flanked by a high column of more than eight metres in circumference one passes into the so-called Hall of Ghosts, thus called because of a delightful arrangement of stalagmites that look like ghosts. This is Hall V, with a very high ceiling and which on the right has a mound which is higher, like a kind of stage. Here, as well as in the former Hall, the ground is flat and of earth and so of great archaeological richness. To the left there are various steps, under a rock overhang, that take one into the Hall of the Cataclysm, the largest of all the Caves.

The entrance is made by going up to point which dominates it completely. The panorama from here is very beautiful. In the middle of the Hall, a large formation sixty metres high by eighteen metres wide, like an anthology of strange formations, rises above another which once probably occupied this same place. Around this great column, an impressive chaos of large blocks, stalagmites and stalactites fallen from the places were they were formed, lean in every direction, offering a strange spectacle of a cataclysm that must have occurred thousands of years ago, as shown by the rupestrian paintings dated at more than 15.000 which are to be found on one of these fallen blocks.

To go through this Hall is for the visitor to see a panorama that has no equal. Its walkways are at different levels so that everything can be seen from every angle.

As in the rest of the Cave, the illumination has been made in such a way that it offers the least possible number of points of light. Coloured lamps have been avoided because, far from enhancing, they detract from the chromatic beauty that some of the formations possess.

All the Halls that can be visited in the Cave are wired for sound, which accompanies the visitor on his round. The accoustics of the monument are unequalled.

Pinochio, detail in the Hall of the Cataclysm

Partial view of the Hall of the Cataclysm

Great Column of the Hall of the Cataclysm

HIGH GALLERIES

At the far end of the Hall of the Cataclysm, going up on the right hand side, and in the highest part, there exists the only communication, that is at the moment viable, with the High or New Galleries. Francisco Navas Montesinos, on one of his explorations, after the Cave of Nerja had been opened to the public, found these Galleries. The entrance to them, so that it can be used as a point of reference, is lit by a red light visible from the bridge of the Hall of the Cataclysm.

A lot has already been said and written about these galleries and a lot more will be. Until now they have been visited only by expeditions of technicians and experts with the sole object of finding a solution to the entrance, either by making it from the outside or communicating it with the part now visited. The topographical elevations realised show differences of height, from interior to exterior, of 80 metres in vertical drop in order to be able to perforate. The studies carried out in this sense, indicate that communication with the actual Cave is not possible: the distance from the first Hall of interest and that is in visitable condition to the so-called Hall of The Cataclysm would mean the blasting of a tunnel that

The Pillards of Hércules in the High Galleries

Cueva de Nerja

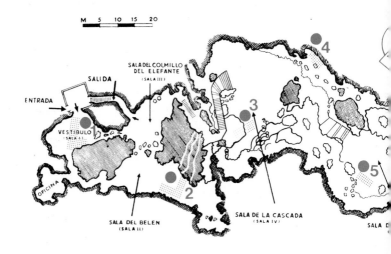

M 5 10 15 20

SALIDA

ENTRADA

SALA DEL COLMILLO
DEL ELEFANTE
(SALA III)

VESTIBULO
(SALA I)

OFICINA

SALA DEL BELEN
(SALA II)

SALA DE LA CASCADA
(SALA IV)

SALA D

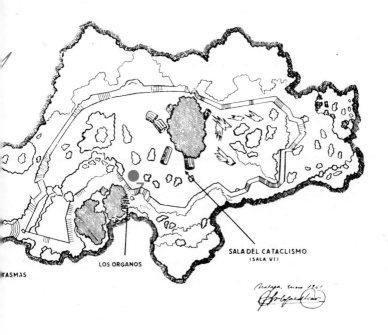

CAVADAS

LOS ORGANOS

SALA DEL CATACLISMO
(SALA VI)

TASMAS

General Plan of the visitable part of the Monument, indicating
the points where archaeological excavations have been carried
out. (See page 54)

would be both long and complicated. This solution is not advisable, independently of the fact that it would not be possible to carry out without affecting the artistic and natural integrity of the monument. Other reasons of a technical nature also impede its realisation. There remains therefore, only the possibility of opening from the outside and a total separation from the Cave now visitable.

The Foundation of the Cave of Nerja, far from abandoning the project, whose difficulties seem to advise this course, given the importance of the necessary work, have not stopped studying the project in the hopes of finding some solution.

We can be sure that the High Galleries have a natural entrance, at present blocked and unknown, and other than the entrance by which they were discovered. This hypothesis appears to be confirmed by the existence of rupestrian paintings, nearly all in one definite zone, and the impossibility that the authors of these paintings could have reached this zone using the present entrance. It appears therefore that there must be an entrance to these galleries through other halls not yet discovered and which made it easier for Paleolithic man to reach this point, as the existence of his paintings makes certain. We know that these artists looked for places that were apart and hidden in order to practice their art, but we also affirm (and I, who write these lines, have proved it) that in order to reach those zones without the resources we have today, of ladders illumination, ropes etc. it makes more than three hours, and one has to pass obstacles that without the help

Hall of the Inmensity. High Galleries

of these materials are unpassable. For this reason it seems more logical to assume the existence of an entrance that the year have hidden. We hope that when we discover, from the inside, some galleries nearer the surface, it will be possible to open them.

To describe a natural monument such as the one that occupies our attention, to attempt to show the beauty of its formations or to compare it with other caves, is somewhat difficult, so I will not do this, but only resume its itinerary, and detail the characteristics which can be considered most useful or interesting.

As has been said before, one gets to these galleries through a small natural entrance which exists high up near the roof of the Hall of the Cataclysm. A series of narrow passages of greatly differing heights, which force one to crawl at some points and to climb at others, reach an all but vertical descent

Hall of the Cataclysm. Partial view

Detail of the Hall of the Cataclysm

which leads into the so-called Hall of the Pillars of Hercules. Near this descent there is a small room where there is one group of paintings. This room appears to form one unity with the following room and it is called the Immensity for its length. Its floor is completely covered with huge stones that fell from what was once its roof and the floor of the galleries which existed above it. There are still some pieces which remain "in situ" like an overhang. Under the mountain of large blocks, at the end of the hall, was found the entrance to another Hall, the largest yet discovered, because it alone is as large as the Halls of the Cascade, of the Ghosts and of the Cataclysm together. It was called of the Lance, because of a huge stalactite, which, in the form of a javelin, is pierced into the ground. At the other extreme, a narrow corridor leads into the Hall of the Mountain, which, without possessing the dimensions of the former, is nonetheless very spectacular and the two are the ones which for their characteristics have most possibilities to offer the public, once they have been prepared.

HABITAT OF THE CAVE

The work of investigation on the area where the Cave of Nerja is to be found is being carried out with the intention of co-ordinating three aspects which are different but intimately interdependant: geological, climatic and biological, so as, in the future, to be able to evolve a coherent theory that explains the evolution of the "whole" and the characteristics of the same as compared to the variables that any one of the above mentioned aspects may have introduced over various thousands of years.

The studies carried out on the geomorphological aspects of the zone that exists in the municipal area of Nerja, and, above all, the evolution of the "carst" in Maro, in order to establish a theory on the genesis and history of the area that can serve as a basis for various future specialised investigations, as well as determining a complete series of technical and geological facts which allow the adaption of the various galleries and halls of the cave for the public with suitable walkways, always protecting the natural formations and within the necessary safety limits for the public, have made it necessary to carry out a bibliographical summary of the various facts known about the zone, which have been elaborated by various illustrious authors as well as a general geological study, which in time can serve as an orientative basis for the authorised colaboration of geologists and specialists.

Some pieces found in the Cave of Victoria, near Nerja

In this way, the actual state of the work only permits the editing of a preliminary report and the bringing to light of what can be considered as a base for future work, together with a series of facts which are considered of interest to the visitor who, as well as admiring the natural beauties, also tries to penetrate a little into the reasons for the formation of this fantastic monument.

The Cave of Nerja is situated within the range of mountains "Cordilleras Béticas", in the zone known as "Bética Sensun Estrictum" also called "Penibética" by a lot of geologists, which runs along the coast from Estepona to the Cabo de Palos. The immediate result is characterised by the amount of material from the Jurasaic and Cretacic ages, both periods falling within the Second or Mesozoic age, and of an antiquity that can be fixed between 150 and 130 millions of years; many examples of the metamorphic fringe, possibly Paleolithic (more than 400 millions of years) exist, more or less affected by the phenomena of metamorphis and of which good examples are to be found in the mountains of Málaga. It is on these materials that are deposited the limestone and calcerous material in which is to be found the cave, and in which, logically, the cathartic phenomena originated its formation. The more modern materials are sedimentary parcels either horizontal or sub-horizontal of the Holocaust or Aluvial Age and possibly the Diluvial (10.000 years) which is limited to a narrow littoral fringe which together with the limestone parcels makes for a sharply contrasted hilly landscape in which are situated the known galleries, without forgetting the possibility of contemporary submarine "carst" and possible communication.

It must be emphasized that in the morphology of this zone the role played by the deep folds of earth is particularly noticeable, as brought about during the Neogenous and the Cuaternarius ages and by the climatic factors, specially eras characterised by a certain aridity.

The cathartic modelling, which is general, is here characterised by forms and details perhaps favoured by the particular privileged circumstances of the zone.

The cavity exists due to three fundamental geological facts: the stratigraphic direction of its lithology; the paleomicroclimate which prepares the rock for the action of water on it, and the descent of the "basic levels". The coincidence of these three factors makes possible our finding halls of such great size, with such a profusion of stalagmites and other wonderful contrasts.

The geological process which originated these formations can be assumed to have started towards the end of the Neocene age, that is to say, more than 12 million years ago, which means to say that the cave was almost as we see it today during the Paleolithic age, in other words from soon after the appearance of man on Earth.

Cathartic phenomena: Calcerous rocks and calcareodolomites are made of calcic carbon, more or less pure, which is insoluble in water. Nevertheless, rain water contains carbon dioxide dissolved from the atmosphere, which originates carbonic acid, capable of attacking the calcic carbon and transforming it into a soluble calcic bicarbonate, as in the following chemical reaction:

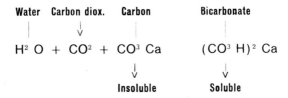

The water is responsible for transporting the bicarbonate. In this way, the calcerous regions experiment an erosion by dissolution and the impurities that are not soluble, which constitute part of the primitive part of the rock, remain "in situ". When there exists a diminution of the amount of carbon dioxide, the result is partial decomposition of the dissolved bicarbonate, giving rise to forms of accumulation, above all in subterranean cavities in which it is easier for there to be changes in the pressure, and, in consequence, variations in the concentration of carbon dioxide.

During its underground course the water of cathartic circulation gives rise to a very special morphology, based on cavities and fillings; it exercises its dissolvent action until it produces caverns and grottes of very different lengths and forms. The most typical examples of accumulation result in stalagmites and stalactites. In the stalactites there exists a form of interior canal through which passes the drop of water, a canal which does not exist in the stalagmite situated underneath; if both forms grow simultaneously, they can eventually join and form a single column.

Piece of ceramic with three handles found on the surface

ARCHAEOLOGY

The discovery of the Cave of Nerja serves to augment the number of important prehistoric beds to be found in the South of the Iberian Peninsula.

The first news of the neolithic in this zone is given by don Manuel de Góngora y Martínez in his publication "Prehistoric Antiquities in Andalucía", Madrid 1968, in which he relates the discovery of the "Cave of the Bats" in Albuñol (Granada), and gives a description of the interesting materials found in the same, amongst which he emphasises the gold diadem, now in the Museum of Granada, and abundant samples of material made from esparto grass, the prototype of the so-called "sandals of hemp", which have been in use, generally in rural areas, until only a few years ago.

In 1884 don Eduardo J. Navarro published the "Prehistoric Study of the Cave of the Treasure". This cave is to be found in Torremolinos, although its exact location has been unknown for years. Its bed must have been very rich in neolithic pottery and anthropological remains.

A few years later, in 1888, the brothers, Henri and Louis Siret, Belgian engineers then domiciled in Aguilas (Murcia) edited in Brussels "The First Metal Ages in the South East of Spain", summarising the most important discoveries made in the province of Almería.

Five years later, Louis Siret published "Prehistoric Spain" and in 1907 "Essay on the Protohistoric Chronology of Spain", and, in the same year, "Orientals and Occidentals in Spain in Prehistoric Times".

Siret thus made a first classification in studying the neolithic in the Southern zone of the Peninsula, establishing three stages which were later reduced to two.

In 1911, the English ornithologist, W. Vernet, discovered the Cave of the Pillar, in Benaoján, near Ronda, a discovery which he communicated to Hugo Obermaier and to Abate Breuil, who went to the newly discovered cave, and, as a result of the studies carried out by these pioneers of scientific archaeology, there was published in Mónaco, under the auspices of the Prince Albert Foundation, the work "The Pillar of Benaoján, Málaga", and which was published in 1915 with all three of their signatures.

This cave was partially excavated in 1942 and offered material analogous to that found in other caves of the littoral: of the Victory, of the Mine and of the Treasure.

Also in 1915, don Miguel Such refers to the Covered Cave of Torremolinos, when recounting the neolithic material found by him. Years later, in 1930, in the Bulletin of the Society of Málaga of Science is published "Advance on the Study of the Cavern of the Hollow of the Mine" about the excavations carried out by the author in 1917 presenting a great deal of precious material, specially neolithic, made up of pottery, bone necklaces, decorations of carved limestone and bracelets of the same material, all forming part of the funeral rights of the human remains found there.

In 1942 don Jorge Rein and don Simeón Giménez

Roof of the Hall of Ballet or of the Cascade

Basin with diagrammatic decoration

Reyna excavate the Cave of the Victoria, and find material analogous to that previously described and which gives evidence of a cultural world of very special characteristics within the Spanish neolithic which has been named the Culture of the Caves.

These caves are only a representative example of those to be found with a prehistoric interest in the area surrounding Nerja. Most of them have been subjected to looting by treasure hunters many years ago. One must add to this that the first excavations carried out in them were not, according to the information we have, made with all the scientific exactitude that such beds need, and that, in some cases, the discoveries described as belonging to them came in fact from the surface or were left behind by previous excavations.

The Cave of Nerja did not escape entirely, at the beginning, from the inevitable search for archaeological pieces, nor did the human remains found on the surface escape the curiousity of the first explorers who, on examining them left some behind and shared out others amongst themselves. It was necessary to track down these valuable materials and proceed to confiscate them so as to be able, in the proper time, to carry out the first study of the bed.

In order to do so, the Provincial Delegation of Archaeological Excavations invited the then Professor of the University of Granada don Manuel Pellicer Catalá, who after his first visit to the bed, and on the site where the first salvaged materials had been laid drew up a document giving his impression of the richness, archaeologically speaking, of the Cave of Nerja, emphasising the importance this monument

59

Pieces of pottery found on the surface

Decorated ceramics found on the surface

would have in adding to the knowledge of prehistory.

The Foundation, on seeing this document, suggested the Professor as Director of the first series of excavations.

The excavations were started immediately; in the middle of September 1959, and after some months of inactivity, they were restarted in May of the following year. In order to get an idea of the whole of the stratification a total of six cuts were made at different points in the Cave, which confirmed, as we shall see later, the importance and richness of the materials contained in this bed for a greater knowledge of the prehistory of the South of the Iberian Peninsula.

It offers a complete stratification which allows us also to place a date on some pieces that came from other caves and which have been wrongly classified, because they came from finds or excavations made under less ideal conditions.

In these cuts one can see levels belonging to the first Bronze Age on the surface (1.800 b. C.) followed by various, belonging to the second Bronze Age, and finally others belonging to the Epipaleolithic.

The second excavation was started on 18th of December 1962 by Miss Ana María de la Quadra Salcedo who excavated in the hall that is immediately next to the staircase that descends to the Cave. Already, on this occasion, we must call attention to the appearance of Solutrensian levels according to the material found and what was said by Miss de la Quadra.

In March 1963 Miss Marina Kleist joined this excavation in order to collaborate with Miss de la Quadra, and who was to take charge of the dating aspect

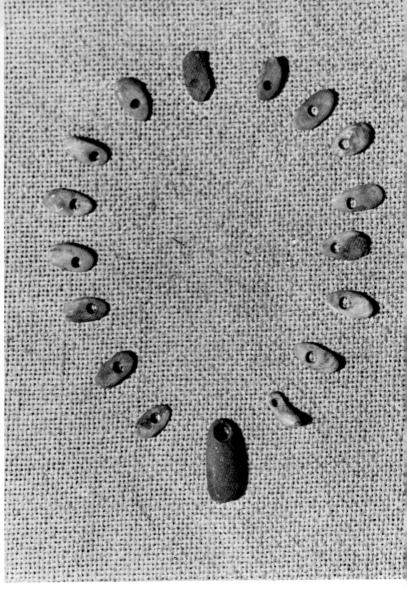

Necklace found in one of the pillars of the Hall of the Cascade

of the excavation. It was on this occasion that the first human remains belonging to the Cro-Magnon were found.

The fourth excavation carried out in June and July of 1965 was made by the Professor of the University of Salamanca Don Francisco Jordá Cerdá. This exploration was started in a passage, not open to the public, that is on the right of the staircase leading to the exit. A great deal of important material, ceramics and other material, gave evidence as to the importance of this zone of the Cave, which, without doubt, was inhabited from the greater Paleolithic until the Neolithic. There still remains a great deal to investigate in this area, as they did not manage to find any sterile stratum.

In September of 1957 the fifth series of excavations was started inside the Cave. Professor Jordá chose the same site for these works in which collaborated the Professor of the University of Granada don Antonio Arribas Paláu and a group of his pupils.

From this year two teams of archaeologists will be formed, one under the direction of professor Pellicer, specialist in the Neolithic Period, and the other under professor Jordá which studied the Paleolithic Age. Professors and students from several Spanish universities will work with them. Work will be centered in the excavations in the so-called "Sala de la Torca", to the right of the exit stairs.

The different excavation campaigns carried out until now have provided considerable Knowledge of human activity and the natural surroundings in which each culture dwelling in the Cave developed. The Cave was occupied continously from 20.000 B.C. until 1.000

ESTRATIGRAFIA DE LAS EXCAVACIONES

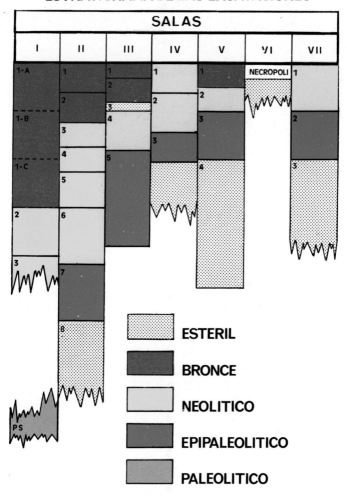

From 1000-1500 b.C. the bottom chambers were used as a necropolis; from 1500-2000 b.C., that is to say, from the Second Bronze to the beginning of the Neolithic, the entrance and the high halls (Nativity) were mostly inhabited. In the Neolithic and Epipaleolithic the Hall of the Cascade was also inhabited. The First Bronze, as the Second, are not so easy to analise. There are elements of Neolithic mixed in with them

Calcium bracelet

B.C. although the former date may be altered in view of future excavations which will certainly penetrate new Paleolithic layers.

This work has for the first time in the Prehistoric surroundings of the Malaga coast, allow us to establish clear differences between various cultures and achieve dating confirmed by C.14 which traces a chronological line situating the Epipaleolithic Era in the 7th. millennium B.C., the 4th., 5th. and 6th. millennium for the Neolithic and the 3rd. millennium for the Calcolithic.

The Paleolithic Era in Nerja shows certain characteristics which are more unique in the "Magdalenian" period of great wealth and importance since they are the only ones in Andalusia, for the moment, and are comparable to the Valencia findings in the Parpalló. The "Solutrian" period has provided rich materials with

Fragments of calcium bracelets

the appareance of human remains belonging to "Cro-Magnon" man.

Another find of human remains, —this time belonging to the "Epipaleolithic" Era—, was made in the excavation of 1982 campaing and it is the third of this Era to be found in the Iberian Peninsula.

Burial place found in the excavation of 1982
in the EPIPALEOLITHIC layer

ANTHROPOLOGY

In the first explorations which were carried out in the Cave of Nerja and in the Hall of the Cascade or Hall No. IV, in a shelter which is situated under the present staircase, fossilised remains were found covered by a layer of live stalactite, amongst which could be distinguished some femurs and a skull, hardly visible, which appeared to have belonged to an adult man.

Advancing further into the cavern we were surprised to see, next to the Ghosts (Hall V) the remains of a woman of some twenty years old, of these remains, best preserved were the femurs, the jawbone and part of the teeth of the upper jaw, which, together with the rest of the skull stood out in a very impressive way, imprisoned in a thick layer of calcium, and which frightened the first visitors. On

these remains there exists now only the bottom jawbone and part of the upper, since the rest disintegrated on touch. It is probably a question of a corpse soaked in water and of which a large part of the skeleton had disappeared. In the ante-chamber of the Cave (Hall I) and imprisoned in the alluvium which closed the entrance were discovered the remains of a boy of about 17 and of which exists the front part of the face caught between the stalactites, to which it is stuck. Naturally this piece, on being found covered with a heavy layer of stalagmite, has not allowed for the corresponding anthropometrical measures to be carried out on it.

When we had the chance to explore the Cave with a little more knowledge of its topography, we found, in a shelter in front of the great column in the Hall of the Cataclysm, a collective burial ground which was found because of the amount of remains of pottery to be seen on the surface.

From this burial ground we have extracted the remains, very badly preserved, of some ten adults and three infants. From this bed came the pieces of most interest, anthropologically speaking, that were first found.

The first of these is a piece of cranium, of which the frontal piece is almost complete, together with part of the right parietal and part of the occipital. It is a shame that this gives us so few clues as to its origin, because, in spite of this, the superciliar arches and the glabular regions, both very prominent, call our attention, and the pointed forehead, the sharp temporal lines and the strength of the bones are very much more in accord with the human forms of the Higher Paleolithic than with the races now known as Mediterranean. This does not however mean that this fragment of skull belongs to an individual of the Higher Paleolithic, since it has now been proved that there is a persistence of paleolithic types which frequently appear in the Spanish neo-eneolithic beds (Jacques in 1887, Scheidt in 1924, Fusté and Fletcher in 1953, Alcobe in 1953). It resembles, above all, the cranium of the "Palafito de Navarres", studied by Fusté, who compares it with the Aurinathian of Combé-Chapele and other paleolithic and mesolithic finds (cranium of Arena Candide, craniums of the grotto of San Teodore, in Mesina, of Les Cottes, of Muge, of Ain Meterchen, in Tunis, of Bobakoy, in Turkey) to which are attributed ties of racial relationship and which have been considered of the same group and as pro-mediterranean by S. Sergi (1950) and Vallois (1953).

Another fragment of cranium, also badly preserved, is that of an individual, probably male, in which can be observed a trepanning located on the upper part of the left parietal, of which one cannot appreciate more than the lower edge and half of the lower arch, since the rest of the skull is missing. It is cut on the bevel and with a sharp edge which indicates that the operation was carried out alive.

Numerous fragments of long bones have also been collected, but they are all so altered by soaking in water and the damp of the cavern that they fall apart on touch and their study is difficult. Other remains are so encrusted in the rock that there they remain, covered in their calcerous layer which makes their study impossible. An example of this are the various ribs and long bones, probably of an arm, to be seen in a "gours" between the Hall of Ballet and that of the Ghosts.

Remains of the Cro-Magnon man

MAN IN THE CAVE

Perhaps the most important discovery made in the Cave of Nerja were the human remains of the Cro-Magnon Age, which were four in number, exhumed during one of the first archaeological excavations in the entrance of the Cave.

The afore-mentioned remains were suitably prepared in order to bear their removal to Barcelona, the city where Dr. Fusté Ara, of the Foundation of Anthropology of that University was to study them.

Unfortunately, the Foundation for the Cave of Nerja only received the preliminary report from Dr. Fusté, as he died shortly afterwards.

The remains disappeared in a fire that took place in the building where they had been stored, and thus all possibility of studying them further was lost.

In the preliminary report here mentioned it was said:

THE CRO-MAGNON MAN OF THE CAVE OF NERJA

"During the course of the last of the four ice-ages which followed each other during the Pleistocene period of the Cuaternian Age, an event of great importance took place: the arrival and proliferation in

Europe of our own species, referred to collectively with the scientific term of homo sapiens fossilis. The patient labours of the pre-historians, paleanthropologists and geologists has permitted us to reconstruct in great detail and which great precision not only the physical and cultural climate in which these precursors of the present race lived, but also their corporeal aspect, in which it is possible to delve only through the skeletal remains, the only tangible evidence left to us. But there is more: the advances of the physics of the Atom have given us methods of dating much more precise than previously, and applicable to different periods of Pre-history. One of these methods, that known as Carbon 14, allows us to antedate the beginnings of the last Ice Age by some 60.000 years; at some 40.000 begin the first cultures of the Superior Paleolithic, of which Homo sapiens was the author, and at some 20.000 occurs the moment that the Cave of Nerja was inhabited by the people whose skeletons now occupy our attention.

One of the races, perhaps the most characteristic, of the humanity of the Superior Paleolithic was, without doubt, man of the Cro-Magnon, thus called because the first skeleton found was discovered in a shelter of this same name, situated in the locality of Les Eyzies, in the French region of the Dordogne. It was there, in fact, in 1868 (very little less than a century ago) the first bone remains were found that gave a name to this fossil race.

Until recently, the finds of Cro-Magnon man made in Spain have been limited to three pre-historic ha-

Remains of Cro-Magnon man

bitats, as: the Cave of the Castle in Santander, and the levantine caves of the Parpallo and Barranc Blanc. Nowadays, thanks to the excavations carried out by Miss Ana María Quadra Salcedo in the paleo-lithic strata of the Cave of Nerja we can dispone of a new find, which is, moreover, more complete than any of the others. And that, not only because of the number of examples exhumed from the said cave, but also because they give us, in spite of the deficient state of their conservation, a much more complete information than the previous finds.

The skeletons coming from this stratum of the Cave of Nerja — which unites to its incomparable natural beauties the tremendous extra interest of having been the shelter chosen by these remote ancestors of modern Humanity — are four in number. One adult man and one adult woman, a child of very few years age and the very incomplete remains of a fourth subject, also adult. The strong pressure to which these skeletons have been subjected, due to the weight of the upper layers and probably also the chemical action of the floor, determined an intense division and alteration of the bones and, in some cases, as can be appreciated in the cranium of the female, also a strong deformation with intense curling of the same, all of which makes for notable difficulties in reconstruction. In spite of this, thanks to the care taken in collecting these skeletons, there are many parts of the same that can be studied, allowing a greater knowledge of their species.

In fact, the reconstruction so far carried out on the same permit us to affirm already, as a definite fact, an important scientific event: the first settlers, which we know of, of the Cave of Nerja, belonged, without doubt, to the ancient race of Cro-Magnon. We refer in reality to Neandertal man, who, in his day, enjoyed considerable diffusion in the levant and the south of the Peninsula, since the remains so far discovered have been found in Bañolas (Gerona), Cova Negra de Játiva (Valencia), Cueva de la Cari- güela in Pinar (Granada) and three places in Gibral- tar. We must admit his presence in Nerja, as this would be proved with only the discovery of some utensil, without human remains, that had been made by Neandertal man.

What are the characteristics that justify attributing the paleolithic skeletons found in Nerja to the Cro- Magnon race? There are various, in effect, that can be distinguished, as the reconstruction of the two adults to which we referred to before is carried out. The most characteristic is the masculine skull, in which one must emphasise a large elongated cranian arch (dolicocefala) with a strong relief in the region situated above the eye-sockets, which is character- istic of the structure of Homo sapiens and which in the Cro-Magnon man was particularly pronounced. Add to this the morphology of the face, low and broad, of flat aspect, with very low eye-sockets of a wide and rectangular outline. The jaw-bone is like- wise characteristic, with a pronounced chin and a mandible line that is low, wide and straight.

Apart from all these characteristics of the cranium, the great height of Cro-Magnon man is well-known, which can be appreciated from the length of the

Excavation in the necropolis of Cro-Magnon

long bones of the extremities. In the feminine skeleton of Nerja we have been able to reconstruct in their entirety the humerus and right hand from whose length we have calculated the height, using various formulan suitable to this. We have obtained a result which oscillates between, according to the method used, 1.57 and 1.65 metres, the most probable results being 1.62 and 1.63 metres which exceeds the stature of the various female paleolithic skeletons with which it has been possible to establish comparisons. A new trait is the curvature, very pronounced, of the "Antero-posterior" of the hand.

An interesting fact, in relation to Cro-Magnon man is that of his persistence in later ages than the Paleolithic, even up to the present epoch. Among the african berbers and the modern population of the Canarian archipealogo, for example, it is well-known that this ancient race of modern man persists, as indeed it does in many places that are pre-historic and neo-eneolithic on the Peninsula. That is also the case in Nerja, where the excavations of the upper levels of the bed brought to light a frontal with similar characteristics as that of the masculine paleolithic subject, and which permits us to assume the persistence of this human form in the later population of the Cave.

This is, today, as much as we can deduce about the subject of the paleolithic populators of the Cave of Nerja, who had the good fortune, as opposed to their more northerly European relations, not only to live in a very beautiful region, where Nature regaled them with a prodigal amount of hunting and fishing for their survival, but where they were also able to enjoy a climate much more benign than that of their more northerly cousins, thanks to their distance from the extensive blankets of ice which covered vast regions of central Europe. In other words, they must have enjoyed even then the principal attractions that nowadays justify the arrival of so many tourists to our incomparable Costa del Sol."

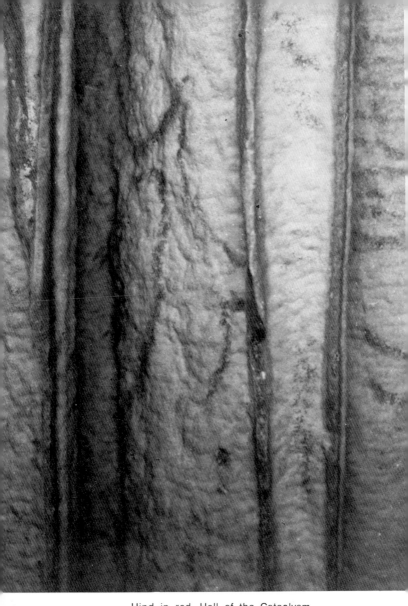

Hind in red. Hall of the Cataclysm

THE RUPESTRIAN PAINTINGS

From the very first moments of the discovery, the explorations carried out in search of rupestrian paintings was a constant labour full of hopeful expectations. The bed found on the surface made for the hope of finding, at least, examples of diagrammatic paintings of this age. It was uppermost in everybody's mind the other paintings found in caves of this littoral. With such hopes predominating no corner was left unexplored.

The result of such a minute search was finding various paintings and many other traces in the following points:

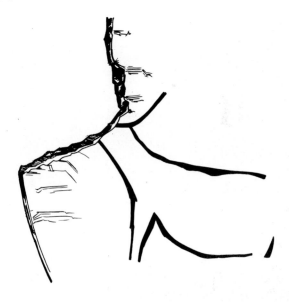

Diagram of a painting in red in the Hall of the Cataclysm

Hispanic Goat (in vertical) Hall of the Ghosts

1.—VISITABLE HALLS

In the Hall of the Elephant's Tusk, on a double column near the present exit, were found some traces of the colour red, almost inapreciable to the naked eye and next to these can be seen a vertical line which looks as though it were made by the nails of a bear in the caverns.

Other paintings were discovered in the passage that exists between the Hall of the Cascade or of the Ballet and that of the Ghosts. In a small chamber on the left, on a large stalactite there is a painting of an Hispanic Goat, in a faded red, in continuous and vigorous lines of some 0.18 cms. It shows the head, the horns, one eye and ear, its back as far as the haunches, as well as the legs and stomach. It is painted from the right, in vertical position, that is to say, with the head at the top of the picture. In front of the snout there are other marks, curves of the same colour, that cannot be identified, and the whole is very blurred as a result of the decomposition of the formation on which it is painted.

The most discussed of paintings, for the importance that it has for archaeology and the study of rupestrian painting, might perhaps be the discovery, on a visit made to Nerja by the investigator Romain Robert, discoverer of the rupestrian paintings of the Cave of Ruffignec in the South of France, which he identified as that of an elephant.

It consists, in a series of lines painted in red, carried out on both sides of a stalactitic protuberance, which, because of its shape, recalls the head of a pachyderm; these lines, symetric of some 10 to 15 cms. long were identified by their discoverer as painted to represent the formation of an elephant.

Other formations nearby show marks and lines of the same colour. They are situated in a small chamber, on the right and in the upper part of the staircase which leads to the Hall of the Cataclysm and very near to those which will shortly be described.

This new group of paintings are to be found in the group of stalagmites, known by the name of the Organ, in the balcony that exists between two staircases, on the way into the Hall of the Cataclysm, on the right. This group of stalagmites in composed of large sheets running parallel and separated by only 0.10 to 0.20 cms. On one of these on the reverse side, at a height of some 1.10 m. from the ground, there is a painting of a hind, in bright red, with a large graceful head and a long neck. The ends of its legs are missing, as also is its head of horns and its nape. Its ears are represented by an elongation of the line of the head, of the back and the neck. As with the previous painting, it is painted vertically, with the head high up and from the right hand side. The size is of 0.25 cms. painted with a line. The dryness of the formation has made for loss of pigmentation, which makes it difficult to find.

Near this paintings, and in this same chamber, are to be found, as in others, marks made in red and black. At the end and on the left, of this same chamber, on one of the sheets there exists another painting. This represents a Hispanic Goat, who has missing one end of its head, the mouth and eye,

Group of fish in red. High Galleries

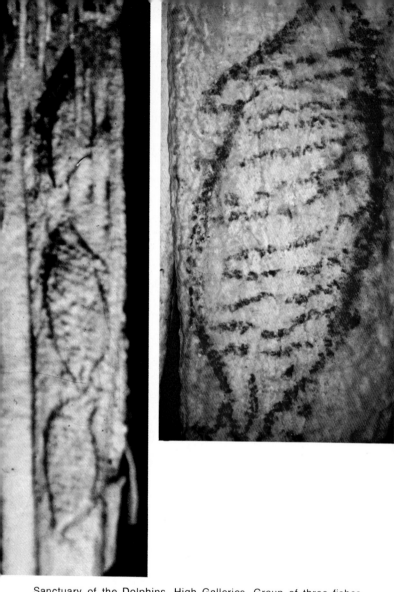

Sanctuary of the Dolphins. High Galleries. Group of three fishes and detail of one

Group of paintings. High Galleries

because of a break in the sheet on which it is painted.

Another group discovered is situated in an inaccessible corner of the Hall of the Cataclysm, on the left of the bridge. On an almost flat surface, which is in reality a large rock, there are some very faded paintings. It appears that they are of a horse, without a head, very like that of the Cave of the Pillar, Benaoján (Málaga), it is of some 0.15 cms. in size. In front of it can be seen the head of a hind of some 0.10 cms. and of a colour ochre, of a very stylised type. Other lines appear to belong to figures now impossible to recognise.

For the moment, these are the pictures found in the visitable galleries of this cave. Two factors combine to make it difficult or impossible to see more:

First of all the dryness of the cavern, which has favoured since before its discovery, the disappearance, by decomposition, of the surfaces on which appear the paintings. The second factor is made up of the hidden places and the difficulty of access which paleolithic man preferred in order to execute his work. For this reason, although the cave has been thoroughly searched, it is possible that some day other paintings may come to light.

2.—HIGH GALLERIES

It is in this part of the Cave of Nerja that the best examples of rupestrian painting are to be found. To see them is not easy, because as has been said before, there exist considerable difficulties in establishing an easy communication with the now visitable part, or an opening must be made from the outside.

The first paintings are to be found relatively near the entrance that leads to the Hall of the Cataclysm and have been carried out on a stalagmite that in its form reminds one of the back of an armchair, and consist of a series of interlinking lines in the form of an arrow, but difficult to identify and black in colour. The second group is on the right of the former, in a zone that is rich in stalactites, forming a positive labyrinth, and in a small chamber which since its discovery has been known as the Sanctuary of the Dolphins. The first figure of this group has been carried out on a stalactite and is the rough plan for the painting of a dolphin, with the head down and a mistake in the third part, red in colour and 20 centimetres long. A little further into the interior and in the same direction is another group, made up of two fishes of the same colour and in identical position and, as in the former, of some 20 cms. long. A third group, the most complete of those found up until now, is drawn very near to the former and nearly hidden by the formations which all but enclose it in a small hole into which the artist must have crawled in order to draw the three fishes and which occupies nearly the entirety of the stalactite on which it is to be found, as with the others it is a vertical position and in red. The first, in the top part, is painted only in outline and measures the same as the others, 20 cms.; the other two are painted in such a way that their tails appear to be superimposed, the one in the centre with the head upwards and the other in opposite position. It appears significant that both show the whole surface of their bodies with fine parallel lines, from back to stomach, in red as the others, and that their size is somewhat larger than the rest of the dolphins here painted, reaching some 36 centimetres in length each.

They are without doubt the most interesting group of paintings discovered in the Cave and the only known representation of dolphins painted in the paleolithic.

Descending from the Hall of the Dolphins down to the so-called Hall of the Pillars of Hercules, and midway towards the Hall of the Immensity, painted on a sheet of calcerous material, which stands out from the wall by some 30 centimetres, are two paintings, one on each side, on that of the right appears the figure of a male deer, painted in red. Its position is nearly vertical, of vigorous execution and it measures 42 centimetres from snout to tail. Only the legs are drawn and the hindquarters are indicated by a line, the horns are simple, without branches, and the eye is well marked, it shows a stretched neck and the head held high as though roaring.

On the other side of the formation there is a painting of a mare with distended stomach, possibly pregnant, although that cannot be certain, since the whole painting is slightly deformed by the necessity of the space available and because of the vertical position in which it is painted. As with the former, it is also painted in red, its lines are fat and neither the snout nor the extremities are finished, and the front legs are also missing. Its length is of 48 centimetres.

Not far from these paintings in another group, carried out on one of the faces of a large fallen block, situated on the left of the same Hall, representing a mountain or Hispanic goat with long horns of exagerated size, one curved backwards and the other frontwards. Strong, sure lines in black, with unfinished legs and tail, it measures 32 centimetres.

Next to this painting appear other lines of the same colour which resemble the head of another goat but without any complimentary details. On top of this, there are other lines in black but which no represent anything definite.

Other paintings in black of pectiform type, in bars, zig-zag and lines exist in other galleries, specially near the Sanctuary of the Dolphins and which appear analagous with those existing in the Cave of the Pillar.

These paintings, according to their style and technique, fit into the Solutran period. The similarity with other paintings in the Caves of the Pillar, of Doña Trinidad, El Higuerón and Los Casares appear to point to a period and culture which becomes daily more clearly defined.

ENTOMOLOGY

This great Cave of Nerja is, according to all the appearances, a "mature" cavern which is fast becoming old and desecated, witness to a basic "karst" which must have been very important in the past and which is still not totally dead.

The conditions of troglodyte habitation in this cave are still favourable to certain groups of insects, although the anthropological action has changed considerably today and will finally destroy them. The cleaning up of the soil together with the strong electric light and the canalisation of the little water that filters in has considerably modified the temperature and humidity, both meteorological factors considered of major importance in subterranean ecology, for which the few cave insects which might be found have looked for refuge in the deepest fissures and holes and are therefore getting rarer and more difficult to find every day.

Using the classic traps of "smooth wells" in different places and with different baits, we have managed to obtain four species of coleopterous, one of which is truly troglodyte and in a subspecific form new to science. The species found are the following:

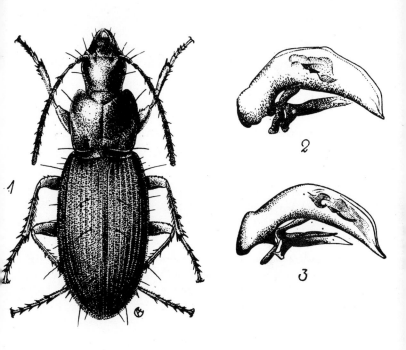

1.—PLATYDERUS LUSITANICUS SPELUS
New Subspecies.

Fig. 1. Material examined: Four females (XI-1960), four males and twelve females (IV-1961). Place: final depression in the Lower Galleries.

After a lengthy study I have reached the conclusion that this coleopterous, the second "Platyderus" that is truly troglodyte known to man, can be included in the group known as "lusitanicus" as a racial form perfectly adapted to subterranean life. For the structure more or less canalised of the inter-fluting elitrals, this form is very like the "saezi" Vuillefroy which together with another unedited race from Almería thus constitute a subgroup of very special facies apparently monofilleted.

2.—PRYSTONICHUS BAETICUS (Rambur)

Six examples captured in the same place as the "Platyderus" and in the same traps (with beer as bait) in the second expedition.

Troglodyte element to be found in nearly all the Andalusian caves.

3.—ATHETA CORIARIA (kraatz)

An example from the Higher Galleries (caught with cheese as bait). November 1960.

Common troglodyte element extended over nearly the whole paleartic region.

Gardens besides Cave entrance

Distribution of the "Lusitanicus Man" in the Iberian Peninsula

4.—CONOSOMUS CAVICOLA (Scriba)

Four examples caught in the same place and with the same bait as the former species.

Troglodyte element frequent in all caves and shelters of Andalucia.

The coleopterous fauna now existing in the Cave of Nerja appears to be poor and has only one truly troglodyte element: "Platyderus lusitanicus speleus" and even this is in a subspecific grade and relatively recent.

According to its distribution, the prototype "lusitanicus" appears to have had its origin in the septentrial half of the Peninsula, or better said, in the mountainous regions of the old Castilian plateau; here the subspecies are much more closely linked (see map on opposite page), are more numerous and apparently less evolved in their external morphology, and certainly ecologically speaking much less specialised. There appears to be no doubt that the said prototype must have been very similar to the f. "Robustus" Mateu, whose adeago is still extremely simple and harmonious.

In order, therefore, to judge by all the philological signs, and ecological and corographical ones, the dispersion of the species must have taken place slowly from North to South, by branching — probably induced by great climatic changes — could have originated on the one hand "speleus" and on the other "alhamillenseis". Having thus clarified the possible procedence and origin of the perfected group "saezi" (characterised above all by the canalisation of the interfluting elitrals), it only remains for us to deduce the hypothetic age of the meridional colonisation carried out by the two new forms, so related to each other.

Above all it is evident that "speleus" and "alhamillensies" are "relics" left over from a wetter geological period — today adapted to biotypes that continue to preserve at least a constant hygrometric grade more or less similar to the primitive one — which is necessary to them: the medium of caverns and damp of the "karst" of the mountains. The emigration of the types or type little specialised must therefore have taken place during the last and great "wurmien" Ice Age which in the extreme South of Andalucia only produced — except on some very high penibetic peaks — a long epoch of relative humidity. The same origin is shared by many other septentrional coleopterous today extinct except in the great Andalusian mountains, as is well known by all specialists.

The rest of the species found in the present grotto are of no great biological interest. They are all cave dwellers at the best of times and common to all subterranean cavities — natural as well as artificial — of the Southern half of the Peninsula. It is, moreover, almost certain that with the re-opening and continual human presence, that the modification of the physical, microclimatic and tropic media, will produce a rapid and progressive enrichment of the troglodyte fauna.

festivales en la cueva

Antonio dancing at the Cave

FESTIVALS

From the 12th to the 14th of June 1960, as the official inauguration of the Cave, the Foundation organised a festival of classical ballet inside the Cave. It was the French company "La Tour de Paris", who staged "Swan Lake" by Tchaikowsky, and it was the first time in the history of the ballet that a work was staged inside a cave. To such a solemn act, the guests invited were personalities from politics, from the arts, as well as critica and journalists of various nationalities who came as far as Nerja for such an historical occasion.

The success of this act was so great that the Foundation agreed to celebrate similar festivals to commemorate, in the future, the anniversary of the inauguration of the Cave of Nerja and as from that date there have been a succession of festivals which have earned a well merited prestige in international circles of the arts.

The main companies that have appeared in The Cave, apart from that already mentioned, are the following:

Ballet from La Tour de Paris. First Festival held in the Cave

Ballet of Tokyo

Ballet of Colombia

Ballet of the Royal Theatre of Copenhagen.

Stars of the Paris Opera.

Antonio's Ballet (*).

Ballet of the Strasbourg Opera.

Pilar López and her Spanish Ballet.

Rafael de Córdoba

Ballet of Monte Carlo

Ballet of the Bucharest Opera.

Luisillo and his Spanish Dance.

Marienma and her Spanish Ballet.

Spanish Ballet of María Rosa (*).

Classical Ballet of Alain Baldini (*).

Silhouette Ballet.

National Ballet of Colombia.

Ballet of Tokyo.

Ballet of Wallonie.

Classical National Ballet.

Spanish National Ballet.

It is difficult to draw special attention to any one of these here mentioned. Each of them was a unique spectacle in itself thanks in part to the incredible natural scenery offered by the Hall of Festivals that on these occasions is lit according to the wishes of the choreographers.

In the interior of the Cave, concerts have also been held. The guitarist Segundo Pastor with the Symphonic Orchestra of Málaga, the National Spanish Orchestra under the direction of Odón Alonso. On other occasions it has been used for films, as that made for Spanish Television, shot for European and American channesl with Antonio, the well-known Spanish dancer and the music of de Falla played by the Orchestra of Spanish Television.

(*) They have performed more than once.

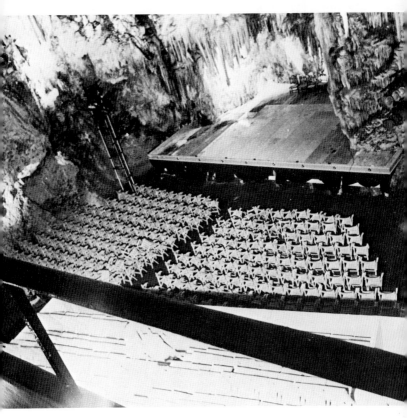

View of the Hall of the Cascade adapted for the Festivals

Their Majesties don Juan Carlos and doña Sofia visit the Cave
when still Princes of Spain

Visit of Queen Fabiola of Belgium

Visit of the former Chief of the State Francisco Franco

Their Majesties don Juan Carlos and doña Sofia during their visit to the Cave

Bay of Calahonda. Nerja

FACTS OF INTEREST

Altitude: 125 metres above sea level.

Interior temperature: 21 degrees centigrade.

Itinerary: Well urbanised and signed.

Visiting days: Every day of the year without exception.

Visiting hours: From 1st of May to 15th of September, from 9h. to 21h. From 16th September to 30th of April, from 10h. to 14h. and from 16h. to 19h.

Bus service: Alsina Graells, with departures from the Plaza de Queipo de Llano in Málaga until the very same Cave of Nerja.

During your visit you can listen to classical music in all the Halls.

All the main travel agencies organise excursions from various points of the Costa del Sol and some of the Andalusian capital cities.

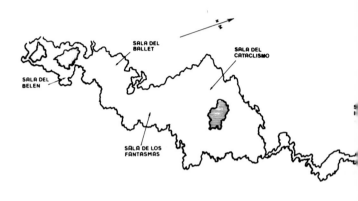

SALA DEL
BALLET

SALA DEL
CATACLISMO

SALA DEL
BELEN

SALA DE LOS
FANTASMAS

1   10   20   30   40   50

Escala Aproximada 1:1000

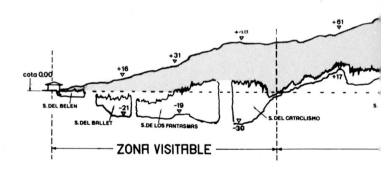

cota 0,00

+16

+31

+48

+61

+17

S. DEL BELEN

-21

-19

S.DEL BALLET

S.DE LOS FANTASMAS

-30

S. DEL CATACLISMO

ZONA VISITABLE

PROYECCION DE LA PLANTA A UN PLANO IMAGINARIO

114

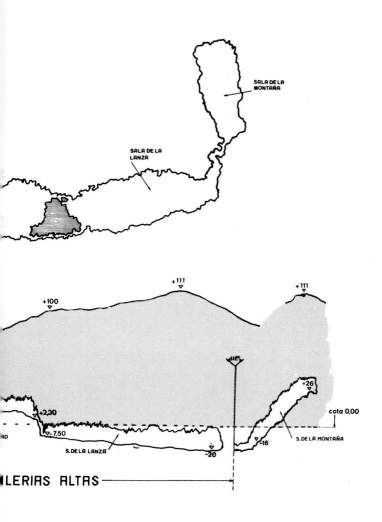

Diagrammatic plan of the visitable galleries and the High Galleries
and a projection of an imaginary vertical plan with indications of
interior and exterior elevations

DISTANCES IN KILOMETRES TO MALAGA FROM THE PENINSULAR SPANISH CAPITALS

Albacete	470	Logroño	873
Alicante	518	Lugo	1.052
Almería	219	Madrid	541
Avila	653	Murcia	440
Badajoz	452	Orense	1.035
Barcelona	998	Oviedo	987
Bilbao	935	Palencia	776
Burgos	781	Pamplona	952
Cáceres	479	Pontevedra	1.136
Cádiz	261	Salamanca	717
Castellón	710	S. Sebastián	1.006
Ciudad Real	381	Santander	936
Córdoba	182	Segovia	629
Coruña	1.162	Sevilla	214
Cuenca	583	Soria	767
Gerona	1.098	Tarragona	902
Granada	129	Teruel	710
Guadalajara	597	Toledo	497
Huelva	305	Valencia	643
Huesca	933	Valladolid	732
Jaén	205	Vitoria	892
León	868	Zamora	754
Lérida	996	Zaragoza	863

INDEX

	Page
Prologue	7
Declaration as a Monument	11
Preface	14
Discovery	18
Geographical Situation	26
Description	30
High Galleries	38
Habitat of The Cave	47
Archaeology	54
Anthropology	69
Man in the Cave	74
The Rupestrian Paintings	83
Enthomology	94
Festivals	102
Facts of Interest	113
Distances to Málaga from the Capitals of Spain	116
Index of Ilustrations	118

INDEX OF ILLUSTRATIONS

Page

View of the gardens 13
Monument 16
View of Maro 17
Prize to the discoverers 19
Works for opening. 20
Photo of historic date 21
Hole made by the discoverers 23
Panorama of urbanisation. 25
Situation plan. 28
Nerja beach 29
Hall of the Narivity 32
Hall of the Ghosts 33
Pinochio 36
Great Column. 37
Columns of Hercules. 39
General Plan of the visitable part 40/41
Hall of the Inmensity. 43
Hall of the Cataclysm. Partial view 44
Hall of the Cataclysm. Partial view 45
Some pieces found in the Cave of Victoria, near Nerja 48/49
Piece of ceramic with three handies found on the surface. 53
Roof of Hall of the Ballet 56/57
Basin with diagramatic decoration 58
Pieces of pottery found on the surface. 60
Decorated ceramic. 61
Necklace. 63
Stratigraphic plan 65
Calcium bracelet 66
Fragments of bracelets 67
Burial place found in the excavation of 1982 in the EPIPALEOLITHIC layer... 69
Fragment of skull. 70
Remains of Cro-Magnon man 73
Remains of Cro-Magnon man 76
Necropolis excavation. 79
Hind in red. 82
Painting scheme 83
Hispanic Goat 84
Group of fish 87
Sanctuary of the Dolphins 88
Group of paintings. 89
Platyderus Lusitanicus. 95
Gardens 97
Distribution of the "Lusitanicus Mann" in the Iberian Peninsula 98
Antonio dancing at the Cave 101
Ballet La Tour de Paris 103
Ballet of Tokyo. 104
Ballet of Colombia. 105
View of Festival Hall 107
Visit of Their Majesties don Juan Carlos and Doña Sofia. 108
Visit of Queen Fabiola of Belgium. 109
Visit of the former Chief o the State Francisco Franco 110
Their Majesties don Juan Carlos and Doña Sofia during their visit. 111
View of Calahonda Bay. Nerja 112
Diagramatic plan 114/115